T0354390

"My Value is Infinite"

Dispelling my adoption perspective and ushering the stigma of the 1950's into modern-day truth, this is Gimmie's story of how love and a sense of belonging can change any journey into a new realization, healing the child within.

The Brightest Star

BALBOA
PRESS

A DIVISION OF HAY HOUSE

Balboa Press books may be ordered through booksellers or by contacting:

Balboa Press
A Division of Hay House
1663 Liberty Drive
Bloomington, IN 47403
www.balboapress.com
1 (877) 407-4847

Because of the dynamic nature of the Internet, any web addresses or links contained in this book may have changed since publication and may no longer be valid. The views expressed in this work are solely those of the author and do not necessarily reflect the views of the publisher, and the publisher hereby disclaims any responsibility for them.

The author of this book does not dispense medical advice or prescribe the use of any technique as a form of treatment for physical, emotional, or medical problems without the advice of a physician, either directly or indirectly. The intent of the author is only to offer information of a general nature to help you in your quest for emotional and spiritual well-being. In the event you use any of the information in this book for yourself, which is your constitutional right, the author and the publisher assume no responsibility for your actions.

Any people depicted in stock imagery provided by Thinkstock are models, and such images are being used for illustrative purposes only. Certain stock imagery © Thinkstock.

Print information available on the last page.

ISBN: 978-1-5043-7767-6 (sc)
ISBN: 978-1-5043-7765-2 (hc)
ISBN: 978-1-5043-7766-9 (e)

Library of Congress Control Number: 2017904757

Balboa Press rev. date: 05/12/2017

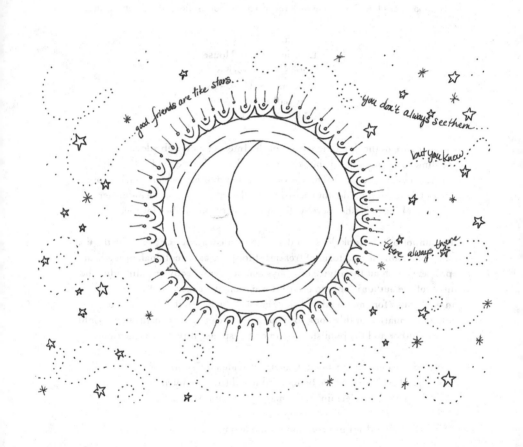

good friends are like stars. you don't always see them. but you know. there always there

For all of the children that have the question "why" in their life and the adults that need to heal the child within, this book is dedicated to you creating your story from where love begins, within your heart.

What you *Create* doesn't have to be *Perfect*

Just enjoy it!

You'll find many Mandalas throughout this story. Carl Jung said Madalas are a "representation of the unconscious self." In addition to making his own mandalas he also incorporated them into his therapy as he believed they were a projection of the psyche and represented a safe place of the mind, and a movement towards growth and healing.

The artwork in this story was hand to pen to paper. It was created from within my heart.

ART DOESN'T HAVE TO BE PERFECT......

But it does have to be FUN!!

The family gathered to celebrate and honor our beloved grandmother, affectionately known to all of her grandchildren as Gim (short for Gimmie). It was Gim's birthday, and we were very excited to have a party just for her.

It is always a fun time when we visit Gim. Laughter echoes throughout her grand, old white house.

That grand house sits on a hill and overlooks the water, with gardens of flowers and vegetables and enormous trees for climbing. The hardwood floors are perfect for sliding in socks, and the banister is wide and can handle two kiddos sliding downstairs as if they are on a toboggan run.

There are big windows, little windows, round windows, and square windows everywhere. The sun loves to send its rays through to shine on all of us.

It is a perfect place to build blanket forts or play hide-and-seek inside and outside.

The kitchen is so big, it echoes when we talk, and it has large counters. While a meal is being prepared, we sit on the counter and watch.

Gim loves to spray us from the kitchen sink hose, inspiring loud shrieks and laughter.

Gim loves music. She likes to play her favorite songs loud, and she grabs a partner to dance and twirl. The music is loud, and so are the conversations and belly laughs. It is a very happy place.

Outside, we play everything from chess to capture the flag in Gim's huge yard. You can always find a pirate up in a tree or a teacher instructing a class on the patio. There is volleyball, basketball, badminton, and always a baseball game.

The cousins choose sides, and immediately the competition begins. Deciding who is safe and who is out make way for discussions of who hit the ball farther and threw it harder.

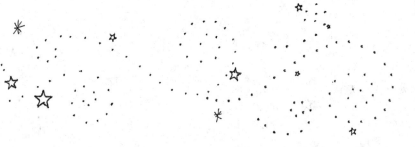

An energy surrounds Gim's house inside and out. All who are there know and feel they are loved.

Gim loves to paint and teaches all her grandchildren on their own easels. They are all set up in her beautiful backyard. She plays her favorite symphony, Vivaldi's *Four Seasons*, while we paint.

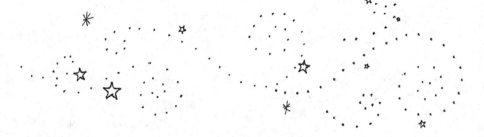

Gim loves to point out the section in the music that sounds like a dog barking. She says, "Can you hear it? Listen real close. Use your imagination, and you'll hear it."

Then she asks us if the summer or winter symphony is playing. Gim says it is important to know the difference. Each of our brushstrokes strikes the canvas with the beats of the music.

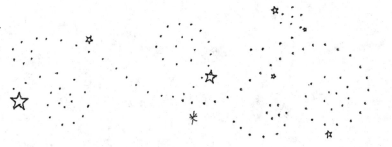

As we are painting, if one of us feels we've messed up and gets frustrated, Gim just smiles and says, "There's no mistakes in art. Your picture wanted to be something different." Then she takes her brush, dips it in paint, and with a few strokes—*voilà!* The painting becomes exactly what it was meant to be. Magic!

In the spring, Gim loves to have all of us help her plant flowers, especially the young ones. She has them take seeds and plant them in special pots. Gim uses her magic metal watering can with a spout as big as a showerhead. We water the seeds with the magic watering can and then spread glitter over the dirt. Gim has them say, "Bibbidy bobbidy boo, make these seeds grow true."

Then it is naptime for the little ones. When they wake up from their naps, something magical has happened. The newly planted pots are full of flowers, and they even have glitter on them!

Gim always makes us feel special. She calls us her shining stars.

Today was Gim's birthday, and we wanted to give her a special surprise, so we made her favorite dessert—chocolate cake without flour (Gim eats very healthy) and homemade vanilla ice cream made with a real vanilla bean. We hid her dessert until after we played our baseball game.

Everyone was ready to play. Even the neighbors joined in. We were a ragtag team. Our uniforms were shorts and t-shirts with numbers we made out of tape. Some of us were short, and some were tall. Some were light skinned and some dark; some had curly blond hair, and some had dark, straight hair.

None of us matched. Gim said, "You are my crazy-quilt family. I wouldn't have you any other way."

It was Jessie's turn at the plate, and just like the other two at-bats, the ball was hit—and it was a homerun!

The score went back and forth, and it was the bottom of the ninth. It was a tied score and Jessie's turn to bat. Jessie's team just knew they would win, and then it would take only moments to run for Gim's surprise birthday dessert that was waiting.

Jessie walked to home plate and got ready. The first pitch was low. The second pitch was outside, and then the next pitch came in. Jessie swung harder than ever before, and *crrrack* went the bat on the ball. Jessie hit the ball farther than it had ever been hit in Gim's yard. We were sure it would land in the stars.

Everyone cheered. Jessie ran around the bases and jumped on home plate. The cousins shouted, picked Jessie up, carried her on their shoulders, and ran to get their ice cream—and, yes, to surprise Gim.

We made Gim sit down and cover her eyes. Out we came with her favorite cake with a big sparkler in the middle, spitting out little stars. We sang, "Happy Birthday."

Gim uncovered her eyes, and her face lit up as bright as the sparkler on her cake. Then we brought out the homemade ice cream. Gim was delighted and said she was very surprised.

The whole family sat on the patio, eating ice cream and cake, which was surprisingly delicious. Lips smacked, cones dripped, and dogs licked faces. It was a messy, happy sight.

Jessie suddenly stood up in the middle of this messy, happy, crazy quilt of a family, and walked up to Gim and said, "Gimmie, I've been thinking about something, and I want to ask you a question."

"Okay," said Gimmie.

"Why was I adopted? Is there something wrong with me?" asked Jessie.

The whole family jumped to their feet, saying, "No! There is nothing wrong with you, Jessie. We chose you to be in our family. We waited and prayed for you! You are ours. We love you!"

Gim reached out her arms and told Jessie to come sit. She said, "I'm going to tell all of you about the story of the Brightest Star." Jessie curled up in Gim's lap, and the rest of the kids gathered around her feet.

"It's a story about how special all of us who are adopted are."

"Us?" asked Jessie.

"Us," said Gim. "I was adopted at birth, just like you, a long time ago."

The aunts and uncles chimed in: "Yeah, a *really* long time ago!" They always teased Gim.

"Up in heaven," Gim started, "there are millions and trillions of stars. You see them every night, right?" Everyone nodded.

"Well, there's one little section of stars that we can't see just by looking with our eyes. The Little Dipper hides this section. Heaven protects these special little stars—not because they're little, but because we're so very special, and there aren't as many of us as the others."

Gim pointed to Jessie and then back to herself. "You and I are two of the Brightest Stars."

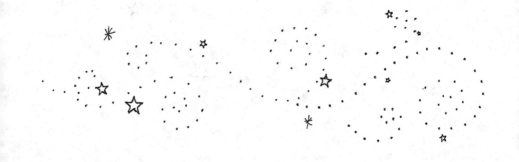

"In this special group, the brightest stars huddle close to one another as they wait until they are chosen for their special mission. It is the destiny of the brightest stars to deliver a message from heaven. Unlike typical stars, the brightest stars have a unique gift of love to bring to the world. When selected, these stars know they're going to a special place that's safe for them until it is just the right time."

"There it was! The bright light shined, signaling it was time to go."

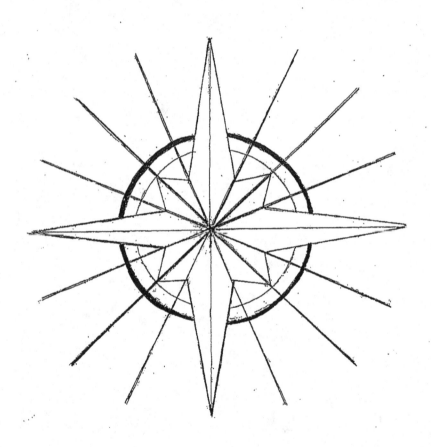

"Shooting through the heavens, the Brightest Star passed through the other stars until finally reaching its destiny. Have any of you ever seen a shooting star?" Gim asked. All of the kids raised their hands.

"The brightest star landed with a *plumpf*, like on a pillow, and snuggled into this new place, exhausted. Then waited patiently for what was next."

"Star slept and slept and slept some more. Days and nights passed by. Then one day, when Star woke up, there were sounds. Star could hear voices and the beating of two hearts.

"It was fun to move, stretch, and play with fingers and toes in this special place. Star felt happy, but still very sleepy."

Sweet Dreams til '

Sunbeams find you

"Star dreamed about what was to come and knew it would be great, magnificent—even spectacular. But when would it happen? I will go back to sleep for now, thought Star."

"One day, Star began to notice that the space that had been so embracing, big, and fun to play in was becoming smaller. Star really needed to stretch out these new, longer arms and legs but could barely move in such tight quarters.

"Star wondered, *How much longer?*"

"Then, one day, the sounds became different."

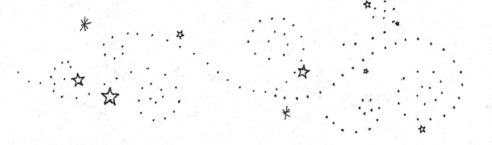

"Star's warm, snuggly home began to tremble like an earthquake. What was happening? The anticipation filled Star with happiness and excitement. Had the special day finally arrived?"

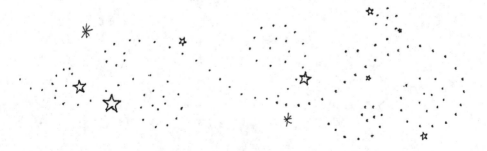

"It is here! Star thought. The day had finally come. It was the brightest star's birthday.

"Star's excitement about meeting the family that was going to love, cherish, and play with Star was electrifying."

Star thought, *Its time to squeeze my eyes tight. I do not want to spoil the surprise of seeing everyone!*

Now, as before, it was time for Star to go. So, head down, arms back, Star soared toward the bright light.

"Star was being born!"

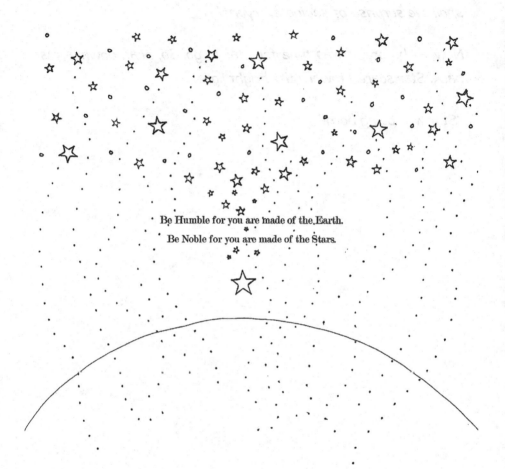

Be Humble for you are made of the Earth.
Be Noble for you are made of the Stars.

"Star had made it! Fresh air and bright lights met Star, and then Star took a breath and then cried and cried and cried and shivered with excitement. The doctor handed Star to the nurses, and they washed Star's little face, hair, and body and then wrapped Star tightly in the softest, most beautiful satin trimmed blanket.

"Star stopped crying and felt safe and warm again."

"After getting Star all wrapped up as snug as a bug, the nurses placed Star in loving arms that were there reaching out.

"Star's eyes popped open to see the faces of this loving family for the first time."

"There they were—Star's family looking back. There was love in their eyes and joy in their hearts.

"Home at last, Star thought as tears streamed down everyone's faces."

"Star was very happy but confused. The voices were different. The feelings of love were strong and felt wonderful but in an unfamiliar way.

"Where am I? Thought Star. Is this my family? Who belonged to the arms that now held Star so tightly?"

"While Star had waited so patiently all of those months, there was another story unfolding. Star remembered hearing the cries and prayers of "what to do" being said by a woman. Star had heard this woman's voice for so long. Where was she now?

"It was starting to become clear. Star was beginning to understand what it all meant."

The hands that

Made the Stars are

Holding your Heart

"With as much love as there was in this woman's heart and with as much strength as her body and mind could find, she had decided to give the Brightest Star the greatest gift she could: life."

"This special woman was chosen to give Star what was needed to be delivered to Earth. Heaven knew she would give the Brightest Star a place to grow and then deliver the Brightest Star to the waiting world.

"It was the biggest decision of her life. It became her greatest gift to God, to the world, and to Star."

Gim paused for a moment then continued. "Star will share the story of a woman that allowed Star to grow inside her, even though she knew that after that Brightest Star took its first breath, there would be another set of arms waiting to embrace, hold, and love Star for the rest of their life. She would have pride in her decision to give Star a better life and would always have a special place of love deep within her heart for Star."

STARS

ARE LITTLE HOLES

IN THE FLOOR OF

HEAVEN

"All of the Brightest Stars know that they were born to one and received by another, as part of their story. It is where their special love started.

"They were chosen to be adopted to show the world that God's love is *in* all of us and *for* all of us. It doesn't matter how we were born, where we were born, or to whom we were born, we are all God's children and all worthy of God's love and goodness."

"This is the special message born within the Brightest Stars, that the world desperately needs. We must fiercely protect these stars, for their message is a cherished gift held deep within only their hearts, locked up for safekeeping, and they are the gatekeepers."

Gim held up the key necklace that hung around her neck and pointed to the key that hung around Jessie's neck. "All of us Stars hold the key," Gim said. "One day, when we feel safe enough and are ready, we will take our exquisite key and unlock our special gift. We will let this beautiful, unique, and special love that only we possess pour out of our hearts like sunshine and embrace the world."

"Star now understood the meaning of the journey. There they were, they had found me! Star thought. This family, whose arms are now holding me tightly, is why I was born!! They wanted me so much that they prayed for me, wished for me, cried for me, begged for me, and now I am here. I am home! They chose me, and I chose them.

"The world so needed me to be born that my birth was out of the ordinary to make a bigger impact.

"Star's eyes were wide open now and could see everyone."

"The smells and sounds were different. Skin colors did not match; eyes were different colors and shapes; and everyone's hair felt different, but none of that mattered.

"They are a crazy quilt of a family, and they are mine!"

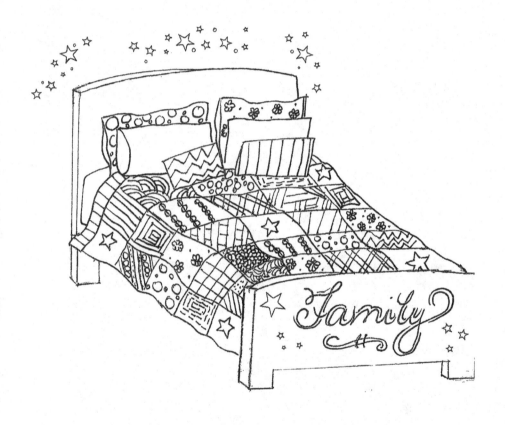

"Star smiled at the thought, *our strong feelings we held in our hearts started from different places but are now connected and are one in the same. We are family. Only our love matters—a love that didn't grow under one of our hearts but a love that grew out of both of our hearts.*"

"I must always remember that I needed to be born, the world was waiting for me, and God loves me and my family— and how special we are. We will all remember with gratitude and love, the woman who sacrificed for me, knowing she would not raise me.

"From this gratitude I will know I was not given away; I was received. I was not discarded; I was found."

"And that's the story of the Brightest Stars. That's our story, Jessie," Gim said.

Jessie hugged Gim's neck and said, "I am very special!"

All of the family members lovingly replied, "Yes, you are!"

Gim had tears streaming down her face, and Jessie asked, "Why are you crying? Are you sad?"

Gim said, "Oh no, sweetie. This was the best birthday I have ever had. I've never been happier or felt so loved."

A Baby is a bit of
Stardust blown from
the Hand of God

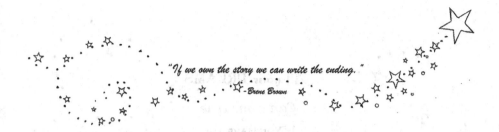

"If we own the story we can write the ending."
—Brené Brown

Let these next pages be the beginning of choosing the Life you want. Write the words you have always wanted or needed to hear. Feel the power of owning your story and choosing the Life you want. Remember you hold the key.

All your DREAMS

Can come true

IF YOU HAVE THE

COURAGE

To Pursue Them

— Walt Disney

Talk to yourself
As you would to someone you Love.

– Brene Brown

"LIFE'S LIKE A MOVIE
WRITE YOUR OWN ENDING
KEEP BELIEVING, KEEP PRETENDING."
—JIM HENSON

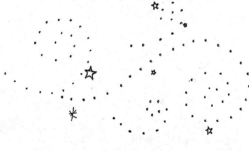

About the Author

I was born in Los Angeles County Hospital one minute after midnight on September 7, 1956, to a single woman who had told her family and friends she was going to the hospital for gallbladder surgery. When her sister found out about the pregnancy, she arranged for my adoption with a couple from her workplace. My adoptive parents were working in the yard of their new home in the "burbs" of the San Fernando Valley when they received the call from my biological aunt about a baby. They brought me to their new home and named me Kim Rae Sparkman.

My wonderful dad loved to tell everyone that he found me under a rock in their new yard. He also told me repeatedly that he had bought and paid for me, so I was a Sparkman. As boorish sounding as these statements were, they gave me the only sense of belonging I ever had. He died when I was 20 and so did the light in my mind's eye.

In the 1950s and 1960s, the term *adopted* carried very heavy connotations. Society branded adoptees as *unwanted, undesirable, bastard, damaged goods, dirty secret, mistake,* etc. These terms caused longstanding damage to those of us adopted in the dark ages. I was the "adopted kid" within my own family as well as my neighborhood. Movies depicted the adopted child in a dark light. Look a little different from others in your family and you are either the mail carrier's or the families best kept secret. Thankfully, adoptions today are born out of a benevolent love, which respects all involved.

The greatest gift I was ever given were my own children, and I have immense pride in my mothering. I would hold my beautiful babies and cry, knowing I could *never* give them away.

So why me? I wondered. *How could my mother not want me?* I could not understand, and it made me question how anyone could love someone that even his or her own mother did not want. My whole life consisted of making others feel worthy and loved; *God put me here to serve people, I could make life better for them than it had been for me,* was my thought process.

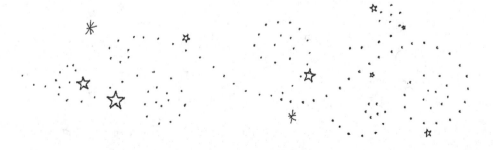

I located my biological mother by chance. (On the other hand, was it?) She was kind, loving, gracious, sweet, and consumed with guilt—a guilt that was always a wedge between us. She gave me life, and I gave her grandchildren. They adored one another. After many years when her health started failing, we moved her across the country to a place close to us. Life events were taking an awkward turn, and I became her caregiver for what was the last six weeks of her life. It became my decision to let her go or keep her alive. The woman who chose not to care for me now relied on me to care for her and to grant her dying wishes. I did what she asked.

She broke my heart a second time.

My aha moment came about five years ago. I was talking to a longtime friend who had three daughters that were adopted. One of her daughters was meeting their biological father, and it was causing much stress. She told me she was thankful she would not have to feel this pain with her youngest since they would never know who the biological father was, she had been conceived from an assault. My response was swift. "We all were meant to be born, and it didn't matter how or by whom." Boom!

I could feel those words come directly from my heart and fly right out of my mouth. I could feel and understand that these words were also meant for me. I too, was meant to be born, and it did not matter how or to whom. I realized I was here for a reason., God does love me, and I am worthy of that love. I am worthy of all of the love in the world.

That realization may sound childish, but the joy I felt was childlike. The screen in my mind went from dark to bright instantaneously as if it was springtime. I knew I was supposed to share my story. I knew my story was not unique to only me. I want to remind (or teach) all of us that were adopted of our worth;

I want to give them their keys.

My original book was titled *I am Not a Mistake.* I attended an I Can Do It event, and Louise Hay signed my title page. I thought this is a fantastic start. Chapter 1 starts with me being given away. In chapter 2, I wrote of being raised by a woman that resented and abused me because I was a constant reminder she could not give birth. Chapter 3, I had to stop writing. I could feel myself going back to a dark place in my mind.

That darkness (one night), was interrupted while I was driving and saw a big bright light in the night sky, a star, and heard the words "heal the children; write a children's book" ringing in my ears. As instructed. I wrote to heal the child within.

I have embraced and allowed the special love we adoptees guard so fiercely to emerge and include *me*, from the place where I now reside. I remember always that I hold the key, and I wear one daily as a reminder.

I know my life purpose, and I adopt it with my whole heart.

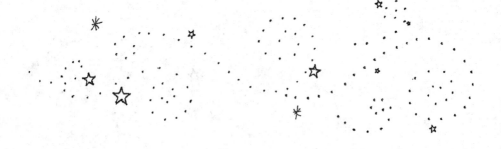

Oh my Stars...

So very THANKFUL

*Several of the Beautiful Mandalas came from mondaymandala.com

Jessie Loehn *NAMASTE*

Colors speak louder than words

Life is about using the whole box of crayons

Listen to the color of your dreams   -Beatles

Add Color to Your Life...

and to this Book

Life is Art Live Yours in Color

Color in a picture is like Enthusiasm in 'Life'

— Vincent Van Gogh